CROSSING THE WATER

Sylvia Plath

1817

HARPER & ROW, PUBLISHERS

New York, Evanston, San Francisco, London

Crossing the Water

TRANSITIONAL POEMS

With a few exceptions the poems in this book were written during the period between the British publication of *The Colossus* in 1960 and before the *Ariel* poems were composed in late 1961. Nine of the poems here were published in the British edition of *The Colossus* (Heinemann, 1960) but excluded from the U.S. edition at the request of the American publisher, Knopf. They are: "Metaphors," "Black Rook in Rainy Weather," "Maudlin," "Ouija," "Two Sisters of Persephone," and five of a group of seven poems published in the British edition under the title "Poem for a Birthday": 1. "Who"; 2. "Dark House"; 3. "Maenad"; 4. "The Beast"; and 6. "Witch Burning." Numbers 5 and 7 of this section ("Flute Notes from a Reedy Pond" and "The Stones") appeared as separate entities in the Knopf edition of *The Colossus*.

The following poems appeared in a limited edition (150 copies) titled *Uncollected Poems,* issued in 1965 by Turret Books, London: "Wuthering Heights," "Finisterre," "Parliament Hill Fields," "Insomniac," "I Am Vertical," "Blackberrying," "Private Ground," "Candles," "A Life," and "Crossing the Water."

"Blackberrying," "The Babysitters," "Two Campers in Cloud Country," "Mirror," and "On Deck" appeared in *The New Yorker*. "Two Sisters of Persephone," "Love Letter," "Widow," "Heavy Women," and "Face Lift" appeared in *Poetry*. "Ouija" appeared in the *Hudson Review*.

Other poems in this book appeared in *Tri-Quarterly, Harper's Magazine, The New Statesman, London Magazine, The Listener, New American Review, Partisan Review,* and *The Texas Quarterly*.

Some of the poems were published in 1971 by the Rainbow Press, London, in a limited edition titled *Crystal Gazer*.

FIRST U.S. EDITION

STANDARD BOOK NUMBER: 06-013366-X

LIBRARY OF CONGRESS CATALOG CARD NUMBER: 71-138756

1 : Wuthering Heights

3 : Finisterre

5 : Face Lift

7 : Parliament Hill Fields

9 : Heavy Women

10 : Insomniac

12 : I Am Vertical

13 : Blackberrying

14 : The Babysitters

16 : In Plaster

18 : Leaving Early

20 : Stillborn

21 : Private Ground

22 : Widow

24 : Candles

26 : Magi

27 : Love Letter

28 : Small Hours

----

29 : Sleep in the Mojave Desert

30 : The Surgeon at 2 A.M.

32 : Two Campers in Cloud Country

34 : Mirror

35 : On Deck

37 : Whitsun

38 : Zoo Keeper's Wife

40 : Last Words

41 : Black Rook in Rainy Weather

43 : Metaphors

43 : Maudlin

44 : Ouija

46 : Two Sisters of Persephone

48 : Who

50 : Dark House

51 : Maenad

52 : The Beast

53 : Witch Burning

54 : A Life

56 : Crossing the Water

CROSSING THE WATER

Wuthering Heights

The horizons ring me like faggots,
Tilted and disparate, and always unstable.
Touched by a match, they might warm me,
And their fine lines singe
The air to orange
Before the distances they pin evaporate,
Weighting the pale sky with a solider color.
But they only dissolve and dissolve
Like a series of promises, as I step forward.

There is no life higher than the grasstops
Or the hearts of sheep, and the wind
Pours by like destiny, bending
Everything in one direction.
I can feel it trying
To funnel my heat away.
If I pay the roots of the heather
Too close attention, they will invite me
To whiten my bones among them.

The sheep know where they are,
Browsing in their dirty wool-clouds,
Grey as the weather.
The black slots of their pupils take me in.
It is like being mailed into space,
A thin, silly message.
They stand about in grandmotherly disguise,
All wig curls and yellow teeth
And hard, marbly baas.

I come to wheel ruts, and water
Limpid as the solitudes
That flee through my fingers.
Hollow doorsteps go from grass to grass;
Lintel and sill have unhinged themselves.
Of people the air only
Remembers a few odd syllables.
It rehearses them moaningly:
Black stone, black stone.

The sky leans on me, me, the one upright
Among all horizontals.
The grass is beating its head distractedly.
It is too delicate
For a life in such company;
Darkness terrifies it.
Now, in valleys narrow
And black as purses, the house lights
Gleam like small change.

Finisterre

This was the land's end: the last fingers, knuckled
       and rheumatic,
Cramped on nothing. Black
Admonitory cliffs, and the sea exploding
With no bottom, or anything on the other side of it,
Whitened by the faces of the drowned.
Now it is only gloomy, a dump of rocks—
Leftover soldiers from old, messy wars.
The sea cannons into their ear, but they don't budge.
Other rocks hide their grudges under the water.

The cliffs are edged with trefoils, stars and bells
Such as fingers might embroider, close to death,
Almost too small for the mists to bother with.
The mists are part of the ancient paraphernalia—
Souls, rolled in the doom-noise of the sea.
They bruise the rocks out of existence, then resurrect them.
They go up without hope, like sighs.
I walk among them, and they stuff my mouth with cotton.
When they free me, I am beaded with tears.

Our Lady of the Shipwrecked is striding toward the horizon,
Her marble skirts blown back in two pink wings.
A marble sailor kneels at her foot distractedly, and at his foot
A peasant woman in black
Is praying to the monument of the sailor praying.
Our Lady of the Shipwrecked is three times life size,
Her lips sweet with divinity.
She does not hear what the sailor or the peasant is saying—
She is in love with the beautiful formlessness of the sea.

Gull-colored laces flap in the sea drafts
Beside the postcard stalls.
The peasants anchor them with conches. One is told:
"These are the pretty trinkets the sea hides,
Little shells made up into necklaces and toy ladies.
They do not come from the Bay of the Dead down there,
But from another place, tropical and blue,
We have never been to.
These are our crêpes. Eat them before they blow cold."

Face Lift

You bring me good news from the clinic,
Whipping off your silk scarf, exhibiting the tight white
Mummy-cloths, smiling: I'm all right.
When I was nine, a lime-green anesthetist
Fed me banana gas through a frog-mask. The nauseous vault
Boomed with bad dreams and the Jovian voices of surgeons.
Then mother swam up, holding a tin basin.
O I was sick.

They've changed all that. Traveling
Nude as Cleopatra in my well-boiled hospital shift,
Fizzy with sedatives and unusually humorous,
I roll to an anteroom where a kind man
Fists my fingers for me. He makes me feel something precious
Is leaking from the finger-vents. At the count of two
Darkness wipes me out like chalk on a blackboard . . .
I don't know a thing.

For five days I lie in secret,
Tapped like a cask, the years draining into my pillow.
Even my best friend thinks I'm in the country.
Skin doesn't have roots, it peels away easy as paper.
When I grin, the stitches tauten. I grow backward. I'm twenty,
Broody and in long skirts on my first husband's sofa, my fingers
Buried in the lambswool of the dead poodle;
I hadn't a cat yet.

Now she's done for, the dewlapped lady
I watched settle, line by line, in my mirror—
Old sock-face, sagged on a darning egg.
They've trapped her in some laboratory jar.
Let her die there, or wither incessantly for the next fifty years,
Nodding and rocking and fingering her thin hair.
Mother to myself, I wake swaddled in gauze,
Pink and smooth as a baby.

Parliament Hill Fields

On this bald hill the new year hones its edge.
Faceless and pale as china
The round sky goes on minding its business.
Your absence is inconspicuous;
Nobody can tell what I lack.

Gulls have threaded the river's mud bed back
To this crest of grass. Inland, they argue,
Settling and stirring like blown paper
Or the hands of an invalid. The wan
Sun manages to strike such tin glints

From the linked ponds that my eyes wince
And brim; the city melts like sugar.
A crocodile of small girls
Knotting and stopping, ill-assorted, in blue uniforms,
Opens to swallow me. I'm a stone, a stick,

One child drops a barrette of pink plastic;
None of them seem to notice.
Their shrill, gravelly gossip's funneled off.
Now silence after silence offers itself.
The wind stops my breath like a bandage.

Southward, over Kentish Town, an ashen smudge
Swaddles roof and tree.
It could be a snowfield or a cloudbank.
I suppose it's pointless to think of you at all.
Already your doll grip lets go.

The tumulus, even at noon, guards its black shadow:
You know me less constant,
Ghost of a leaf, ghost of a bird.
I circle the writhen trees. I am too happy.
These faithful dark-boughed cypresses

Brood, rooted in their heaped losses.
Your cry fades like the cry of a gnat.
I lose sight of you on your blind journey,
While the heath grass glitters and the spindling rivulets
Unspool and spend themselves. My mind runs with them,

Pooling in heel-prints, fumbling pebble and stem.
The day empties its images
Like a cup or a room. The moon's crook whitens,
Thin as the skin seaming a scar.
Now, on the nursery wall,

The blue night plants, the little pale blue hill
In your sister's birthday picture start to glow.
The orange pompons, the Egyptian papyrus
Light up. Each rabbit-eared
Blue shrub behind the glass
Exhales an indigo nimbus,

A sort of cellophane balloon.
The old dregs, the old difficulties take me to wife.
Gulls stiffen to their chill vigil in the drafty half-light;
I enter the lit house.

Heavy Women

Irrefutable, beautifully smug
As Venus, pedestalled on a half-shell
Shawled in blond hair and the salt
Scrim of a sea breeze, the women
Settle in their belling dresses.
Over each weighty stomach a face
Floats calm as a moon or a cloud.

Smiling to themselves, they meditate
Devoutly as the Dutch bulb
Forming its twenty petals.
The dark still nurses its secret.
On the green hill, under the thorn trees,
They listen for the millennium,
The knock of the small, new heart.

Pink-buttocked infants attend them.
Looping wool, doing nothing in particular,
They step among the archetypes.
Dusk hoods them in Mary-blue
While far off, the axle of winter
Grinds round, bearing down with the straw,
The star, the wise grey men.

Insomniac

The night sky is only a sort of carbon paper,
Blueblack, with the much-poked periods of stars
Letting in the light, peephole after peephole—
A bonewhite light, like death, behind all things.
Under the eyes of the stars and the moon's rictus
He suffers his desert pillow, sleeplessness
Stretching its fine, irritating sand in all directions.

Over and over the old, granular movie
Exposes embarrassments—the mizzling days
Of childhood and adolescence, sticky with dreams,
Parental faces on tall stalks, alternately stern and tearful,
A garden of buggy rose that made him cry.
His forehead is bumpy as a sack of rocks.
Memories jostle each other for face-room like obsolete film stars.

He is immune to pills: red, purple, blue—
How they lit the tedium of the protracted evening!
Those sugary planets whose influence won for him
A life baptized in no-life for a while,
And the sweet, drugged waking of a forgetful baby.
Now the pills are worn-out and silly, like classical gods.
Their poppy-sleepy colors do him no good.

His head is a little interior of grey mirrors.
Each gesture flees immediately down an alley
Of diminishing perspectives, and its significance
Drains like water out the hole at the far end.
He lives without privacy in a lidless room,
The bald slots of his eyes stiffened wide-open
On the incessant heat-lightning flicker of situations.

Nightlong, in the granite yard, invisible cats
Have been howling like women, or damaged instruments.
Already he can feel daylight, his white disease,
Creeping up with her hatful of trivial repetitions.
The city is a map of cheerful twitters now,
And everywhere people, eyes mica-silver and blank,
Are riding to work in rows, as if recently brainwashed.

I Am Vertical

But I would rather be horizontal.
I am not a tree with my root in the soil
Sucking up minerals and motherly love
So that each March I may gleam into leaf,
Nor am I the beauty of a garden bed
Attracting my share of Ahs and spectacularly painted,
Unknowing I must soon unpetal.
Compared with me, a tree is immortal
And a flower-head not tall, but more startling,
And I want the one's longevity and the other's daring.

Tonight, in the infinitesimal light of the stars,
The trees and flowers have been strewing their cool odors.
I walk among them, but none of them are noticing.
Sometimes I think that when I am sleeping
I must most perfectly resemble them—
Thoughts gone dim.
It is more natural to me, lying down.
Then the sky and I are in open conversation,
And I shall be useful when I lie down finally:
Then the trees may touch me for once, and the flowers have
       time for me.

Blackberrying

Nobody in the lane, and nothing, nothing but blackberries,
Blackberries on either side, though on the right mainly,
A blackberry alley, going down in hooks, and a sea
Somewhere at the end of it, heaving. Blackberries
Big as the ball of my thumb, and dumb as eyes
Ebon in the hedges, fat
With blue-red juices. These they squander on my fingers.
I had not asked for such a blood sisterhood; they must love me.
They accommodate themselves to my milkbottle, flattening
          their sides.

Overhead go the choughs in black, cacophonous flocks—
Bits of burnt paper wheeling in a blown sky.
Theirs is the only voice, protesting, protesting.
I do not think the sea will appear at all.
The high, green meadows are glowing, as if lit from within.
I come to one bush of berries so ripe it is a bush of flies,
Hanging their blue-green bellies and their wing panes in a
          Chinese screen.
The honey-feast of the berries has stunned them; they believe
          in heaven.
One more hook, and the berries and bushes end.

The only thing to come now is the sea.
From between two hills a sudden wind funnels at me,
Slapping its phantom laundry in my face.
These hills are too green and sweet to have tasted salt.
I follow the sheep path between them. A last hook brings me
To the hills' northern face, and the face is orange rock
That looks out on nothing, nothing but a great space
Of white and pewter lights, and a din like silversmiths
Beating and beating at an intractable metal.

The Babysitters

It is ten years, now, since we rowed to Children's Island.
The sun flamed straight down that noon on the water off
        Marblehead.
That summer we wore black glasses to hide our eyes.
We were always crying, in our spare rooms, little put-upon
        sisters,
In the two, huge, white, handsome houses in Swampscott.
When the sweetheart from England appeared, with her cream
        skin and Yardley cosmetics,
I had to sleep in the same room with the baby on a too-short cot,
And the seven-year-old wouldn't go out unless his jersey stripes
Matched the stripes of his socks.

O it was richness!—eleven rooms and a yacht
With a polished mahogany stair to let into the water
And a cabin boy who could decorate cakes in six-colored
        frosting.   .
But I didn't know how to cook, and babies depressed me.
Nights, I wrote in my diary spitefully, my fingers red
With triangular scorch marks from ironing tiny ruchings and
        puffed sleeves.
When the sporty wife and her doctor husband went on one of
        their cruises
They left me a borrowed maid named Ellen, "for protection,"
And a small Dalmatian.

In your house, the main house, you were better off.
You had a rose garden and a guest cottage and a model
        apothecary shop
And a cook and a maid, and knew about the key to the bourbon.
I remember you playing "Ja-Da" in a pink piqué dress
On the game-room piano, when the "big people" were out,

And the maid smoked and shot pool under a green-shaded lamp.
The cook had one walleye and couldn't sleep, she was so
        nervous.
On trial, from Ireland, she burned batch after batch of cookies
Till she was fired.

O what has come over us, my sister!
On that day-off the two of us cried so hard to get
We lifted a sugared ham and a pineapple from the grownups'
        icebox
And rented an old green boat. I rowed. You read
Aloud, cross-legged on the stern seat, from the *Generation of
        Vipers*.
So we bobbed out to the island. It was deserted—
A gallery of creaking porches and still interiors,
Stopped and awful as a photograph of somebody laughing,
But ten years dead.

The bold gulls dove as if they owned it all.
We picked up sticks of driftwood and beat them off,
Then stepped down the steep beach shelf and into the water.
We kicked and talked. The thick salt kept us up.
I see us floating there yet, inseparable—two cork dolls.
What keyhole have we slipped through, what door has shut?
The shadows of the grasses inched round like hands of a clock,
And from our opposite continents we wave and call.
Everything has happened.

In Plaster

I shall never get out of this! There are two of me now:
This new absolutely white person and the old yellow one,
And the white person is certainly the superior one.
She doesn't need food, she is one of the real saints.
At the beginning I hated her, she had no personality—
She lay in bed with me like a dead body
And I was scared, because she was shaped just the way I was

Only much whiter and unbreakable and with no complaints.
I couldn't sleep for a week, she was so cold.
I blamed her for everything, but she didn't answer.
I couldn't understand her stupid behavior!
When I hit her she held still, like a true pacifist.
Then I realized what she wanted was for me to love her:
She began to warm up, and I saw her advantages.

Without me, she wouldn't exist, so of course she was grateful.
I gave her a soul, I bloomed out of her as a rose
Blooms out of a vase of not very valuable porcelain,
And it was I who attracted everybody's attention,
Not her whiteness and beauty, as I had at first supposed.
I patronized her a little, and she lapped it up—
You could tell almost at once she had a slave mentality.

I didn't mind her waiting on me, and she adored it.
In the morning she woke me early, reflecting the sun
From her amazingly white torso, and I couldn't help but notice
Her tidiness and her calmness and her patience:
She humored my weakness like the best of nurses,
Holding my bones in place so they would mend properly.
In time our relationship grew more intense.

She stopped fitting me so closely and seemed offish.
I felt her criticizing me in spite of herself,
As if my habits offended her in some way.
She let in the drafts and became more and more absent-minded.
And my skin itched and flaked away in soft pieces
Simply because she looked after me so badly.
Then I saw what the trouble was: she thought she was immortal.

She wanted to leave me, she thought she was superior,
And I'd been keeping her in the dark, and she was resentful—
Wasting her days waiting on a half-corpse!
And secretly she began to hope I'd die.
Then she could cover my mouth and eyes, cover me entirely,
And wear my painted face the way a mummy-case
Wears the face of a pharaoh, though it's made of mud and water.

I wasn't in any position to get rid of her.
She'd supported me for so long I was quite limp—
I had even forgotten how to walk or sit,
So I was careful not to upset her in any way
Or brag ahead of time how I'd avenge myself.
Living with her was like living with my own coffin:
Yet I still depended on her, though I did it regretfully.

I used to think we might make a go of it together—
After all, it was a kind of marriage, being so close.
Now I see it must be one or the other of us.
She may be a saint, and I may be ugly and hairy,
But she'll soon find out that that doesn't matter a bit.
I'm collecting my strength; one day I shall manage without her,
And she'll perish with emptiness then, and begin to miss me.

Leaving Early

Lady, your room is lousy with flowers.
When you kick me out, that's what I'll remember,
Me, sitting here bored as a leopard
In your jungle of wine-bottle lamps,
Velvet pillows the color of blood pudding
And the white china flying fish from Italy.
I forget you, hearing the cut flowers
Sipping their liquids from assorted pots,
Pitchers and Coronation goblets
Like Monday drunkards. The milky berries
Bow down, a local constellation,
Toward their admirers in the tabletop:
Mobs of eyeballs looking up.
Are those petals or leaves you've paired them with—
Those green-striped ovals of silver tissue?
The red geraniums I know.
Friends, friends. They stink of armpits
And the involved maladies of autumn,
Musky as a lovebed the morning after.
My nostrils prickle with nostalgia.
Henna hags: cloth of your cloth.
They toe old water thick as fog.

The roses in the Toby jug
Gave up the ghost last night. High time.
Their yellow corsets were ready to split.
You snored, and I heard the petals unlatch,
Tapping and ticking like nervous fingers.
You should have junked them before they died.
Daybreak discovered the bureau lid
Littered with Chinese hands. Now I'm stared at
By chrysanthemums the size

Of Holofernes' head, dipped in the same
Magenta as this fubsy sofa.
In the mirror their doubles back them up.
Listen: your tenant mice
Are rattling the cracker packets. Fine flour
Muffles their bird feet: they whistle for joy.
And you doze on, nose to the wall.
This mizzle fits me like a sad jacket.
How did we make it up to your attic?
You handed me gin in a glass bud vase.
We slept like stones. Lady, what am I doing
With a lung full of dust and a tongue of wood,
Knee-deep in the cold and swamped by flowers?

Stillborn

These poems do not live: it's a sad diagnosis.
They grew their toes and fingers well enough,
Their little foreheads bulged with concentration.
If they missed out on walking about like people
It wasn't for any lack of mother love.

O I cannot understand what happened to them!
They are proper in shape and number and every part.
They sit so nicely in the pickling fluid!
They smile and smile and smile and smile at me.
And still the lungs won't fill and the heart won't start.

They are not pigs, they are not even fish,
Though they have a piggy and a fishy air—
It would be better if they were alive, and that's what they were.
But they are dead, and their mother near dead with distraction,
And they stupidly stare, and do not speak of her.

Private Ground

First frost, and I walk among the rose-fruit, the marble toes
Of the Greek beauties you brought
Off Europe's relic heap
To sweeten your neck of the New York woods.
Soon each white lady will be boarded up
Against the cracking climate.

All morning, with smoking breath, the handyman
Has been draining the goldfish ponds.
They collapse like lungs, the escaped water
Threading back, filament by filament, to the pure
Platonic table where it lives. The baby carp
Litter the mud like orangepeel.

Eleven weeks, and I know your estate so well
I need hardly go out at all.
A superhighway seals me off.
Trading their poisons, the north and south bound cars
Flatten the doped snakes to ribbon. In here, the grasses
Unload their griefs on my shoes,

The woods creak and ache, and the day forgets itself.
I bend over this drained basin where the small fish
Flex as the mud freezes.
They glitter like eyes, and I collect them all.
Morgue of old logs and old images, the lake
Opens and shuts, accepting them among its reflections.

Widow

Widow. The word consumes itself—
Body, a sheet of newsprint on the fire
Levitating a numb minute in the updraft
Over the scalding, red topography
That will put her heart out like an only eye.

Widow. The dead syllable, with its shadow
Of an echo, exposes the panel in the wall
Behind which the secret passage lies—stale air,
Fusty remembrances, the coiled-spring stair
That opens at the top onto nothing at all. . . .

Widow. The bitter spider sits
And sits in the center of her loveless spokes.
Death is the dress she wears, her hat and collar.
The moth-face of her husband, moonwhite and ill,
Circles her like a prey she'd love to kill

A second time, to have him near again—
A paper image to lay against her heart
The way she laid his letters, till they grew warm
And seemed to give her warmth, like a live skin.
But it is she who is paper now, warmed by no one.

Widow: that great, vacant estate!
The voice of God is full of draftiness,
Promising simply the hard stars, the space
Of immortal blankness between stars
And no bodies, singing like arrows up to heaven.

Widow, the compassionate trees bend in,
The trees of loneliness, the trees of mourning.
They stand like shadows about the green landscape—
Or even like black holes cut out of it.
A widow resembles them, a shadow-thing,

Hand folding hand, and nothing in between.
A bodiless soul could pass another soul
In this clear air and never notice it—
One soul pass through the other, frail as smoke
And utterly ignorant of the way it took.

That is the fear she has—the fear
His soul may beat and be beating at her dull sense
Like blue Mary's angel, dovelike against a pane
Blinded to all but the grey, spiritless room
It looks in on, and must go on looking in on.

Candles

They are the last romantics, these candles:
Upside-down hearts of light tipping wax fingers,
And the fingers, taken in by their own haloes,
Grown milky, almost clear, like the bodies of saints.
It is touching, the way they'll ignore

A whole family of prominent objects
Simply to plumb the deeps of an eye
In its hollow of shadows, its fringe of reeds,
And the owner past thirty, no beauty at all.
Daylight would be more judicious,

Giving everybody a fair hearing.
They should have gone out with balloon flights and
        the stereopticon.
This is no time for the private point of view.
When I light them, my nostrils prickle.
Their pale, tentative yellows

Drag up false, Edwardian sentiments,
And I remember my maternal grandmother from Vienna.
As a schoolgirl she gave roses to Franz Josef.
The burghers sweated and wept. The children wore white.
And my grandfather moped in the Tyrol,

Imagining himself a headwaiter in America,
Floating in a high-church hush
Among ice buckets, frosty napkins.
These little globes of light are sweet as pears.
Kindly with invalids and mawkish women,

They mollify the bald moon.
Nun-souled, they burn heavenward and never marry.
The eyes of the child I nurse are scarcely open.
In twenty years I shall be retrograde
As these drafty ephemerids.

I watch their spilt tears cloud and dull to pearls.
How shall I tell anything at all
To this infant still in a birth-drowse?
Tonight, like a shawl, the mild light enfolds her,
The shadows stoop over like guests at a christening.

Magi

The abstracts hover like dull angels:
Nothing so vulgar as a nose or an eye
Bossing the ethereal blanks of their face-ovals.

Their whiteness bears no relation to laundry,
Snow, chalk or suchlike. They're
The real thing, all right: the Good, the True—

Salutary and pure as boiled water,
Loveless as the multiplication table.
While the child smiles into thin air.

Six months in the world, and she is able
To rock on all fours like a padded hammock.
For her, the heavy notion of Evil

Attending her cot is less than a bellyache,
And Love the mother of milk, no theory.
They mistake their star, these papery godfolk.

They want the crib of some lamp-headed Plato.
Let them astound his heart with their merit.
What girl ever flourished in such company?

Love Letter

Not easy to state the change you made.
If I'm alive now, then I was dead,
Though, like a stone, unbothered by it,
Staying put according to habit.
You didn't just toe me an inch, no—
Nor leave me to set my small bald eye
Skyward again, without hope, of course,
Of apprehending blueness, or stars.

That wasn't it. I slept, say: a snake
Masked among black rocks as a black rock
In the white hiatus of winter—
Like my neighbors, taking no pleasure
In the million perfectly chiseled
Cheeks alighting each moment to melt
My cheek of basalt. They turned to tears,
Angels weeping over dull natures,
But didn't convince me. Those tears froze.
Each dead head had a visor of ice.

And I slept on like a bent finger.
The first thing I saw was sheer air
And the locked drops rising in a dew
Limpid as spirits. Many stones lay
Dense and expressionless round about.
I didn't know what to make of it.
I shone, mica-scaled, and unfolded
To pour myself out like a fluid
Among bird feet and the stems of plants.
I wasn't fooled. I knew you at once.

Tree and stone glittered, without shadows.
My finger-length grew lucent as glass.
I started to bud like a March twig:
An arm and a leg, an arm, a leg.
From stone to cloud, so I ascended.
Now I resemble a sort of god
Floating through the air in my soul-shift
Pure as a pane of ice. It's a gift.

Small Hours

Empty, I echo to the least footfall,
Museum without statues, grand with pillars, porticoes, rotundas.
In my courtyard a fountain leaps and sinks back into itself,
Nun-hearted and blind to the world. Marble lilies
Exhale their pallor like scent.

I imagine myself with a great public,
Mother of a white Nike and several bald-eyed Apollos.
Instead, the dead injure me with attentions, and nothing
        can happen.
The moon lays a hand on my forehead,
Blank-faced and mum as a nurse.

Sleep in the Mojave Desert

Out here there are no hearthstones,
Hot grains, simply. It is dry, dry.
And the air dangerous. Noonday acts queerly
On the mind's eye, erecting a line
Of poplars in the middle distance, the only
Object beside the mad, straight road
One can remember men and houses by.
A cool wind should inhabit those leaves
And a dew collect on them, dearer than money,
In the blue hour before sunup.
Yet they recede, untouchable as tomorrow,
Or those glittery fictions of spilt water
That glide ahead of the very thirsty.

I think of the lizards airing their tongues
In the crevice of an extremely small shadow
And the toad guarding his heart's droplet.
The desert is white as a blind man's eye,
Comfortless as salt. Snake and bird
Doze behind the old masks of fury.
We swelter like firedogs in the wind.
The sun puts its cinder out. Where we lie
The heat-cracked crickets congregate
In their black armorplate and cry.
The day-moon lights up like a sorry mother,
And the crickets come creeping into our hair
To fiddle the short night away.

The Surgeon at 2 A.M.

The white light is artificial, and hygienic as heaven.
The microbes cannot survive it.
They are departing in their transparent garments, turned aside
From the scalpels and the rubber hands.
The scalded sheet is a snowfield, frozen and peaceful.
The body under it is in my hands.
As usual there is no face. A lump of Chinese white
With seven holes thumbed in. The soul is another light.
I have not seen it; it does not fly up.
Tonight it has receded like a ship's light.

It is a garden I have to do with—tubers and fruits
Oozing their jammy substances,
A mat of roots. My assistants hook them back.
Stenches and colors assail me.
This is the lung-tree.
These orchids are splendid. They spot and coil like snakes.
The heart is a red bell-bloom, in distress.
I am so small
In comparison to these organs!
I worm and hack in a purple wilderness.

The blood is a sunset. I admire it.
I am up to my elbows in it, red and squeaking.
Still it seeps up, it is not exhausted.
So magical! A hot spring
I must seal off and let fill
The intricate, blue piping under this pale marble.
How I admire the Romans—
Aqueducts, the Baths of Caracalla, the eagle nose!
The body is a Roman thing.
It has shut its mouth on the stone pill of repose.

30

It is a statue the orderlies are wheeling off.
I have perfected it.
I am left with an arm or a leg,
A set of teeth, or stones
To rattle in a bottle and take home,
And tissues in slices—a pathological salami.
Tonight the parts are entombed in an icebox.
Tomorrow they will swim
In vinegar like saints' relics.
Tomorrow the patient will have a clean, pink plastic limb.

Over one bed in the ward, a small blue light
Announces a new soul. The bed is blue.
Tonight, for this person, blue is a beautiful color.
The angels of morphia have borne him up.
He floats an inch from the ceiling,
Smelling the dawn drafts.
I walk among sleepers in gauze sarcophagi.
The red night lights are flat moons. They are dull with blood.
I am the sun, in my white coat,
Grey faces, shuttered by drugs, follow me like flowers.

Two Campers in Cloud Country

(ROCK LAKE, CANADA)

In this country there is neither measure nor balance
To redress the dominance of rocks and woods,
The passage, say, of these man-shaming clouds.

No gesture of yours or mine could catch their attention,
No word make them carry water or fire the kindling
Like local trolls in the spell of a superior being.

Well, one wearies of the Public Gardens: one wants a vacation
Where trees and clouds and animals pay no notice;
Away from the labeled elms, the tame tea-roses.

It took three days driving north to find a cloud
The polite skies over Boston couldn't possibly accommodate.
Here on the last frontier of the big, brash spirit

The horizons are too far off to be chummy as uncles;
The colors assert themselves with a sort of vengeance.
Each day concludes in a huge splurge of vermilions

And night arrives in one gigantic step.
It is comfortable, for a change, to mean so little.
These rocks offer no purchase to herbage or people:

They are conceiving a dynasty of perfect cold.
In a month we'll wonder what plates and forks are for.
I lean to you, numb as a fossil. Tell me I'm here.

The Pilgrims and Indians might never have happened.
Planets pulse in the lake like bright amoebas;
The pines blot our voices up in their lightest sighs.

Around our tent the old simplicities sough
Sleepily as Lethe, trying to get in.
We'll wake blank-brained as water in the dawn.

Mirror

I am silver and exact. I have no preconceptions.
Whatever I see I swallow immediately
Just as it is, unmisted by love or dislike.
I am not cruel, only truthful—
The eye of a little god, four-cornered.
Most of the time I meditate on the opposite wall.
It is pink, with speckles. I have looked at it so long
I think it is a part of my heart. But it flickers.
Faces and darkness separate us over and over.

Now I am a lake. A woman bends over me,
Searching my reaches for what she really is.
Then she turns to those liars, the candles or the moon.
I see her back, and reflect it faithfully.
She rewards me with tears and an agitation of hands.
I am important to her. She comes and goes.
Each morning it is her face that replaces the darkness.
In me she has drowned a young girl, and in me an old woman
Rises toward her day after day, like a terrible fish.

On Deck

Midnight in the mid-Atlantic. On deck.
Wrapped up in themselves as in thick veiling
And mute as mannequins in a dress shop,
Some few passengers keep track
Of the old star-map on the ceiling.
Tiny and far, a single ship

Lit like a two-tiered wedding cake
Carries its candles slowly off.
Now there is nothing much to look at.
Still nobody will move or speak—
The bingo players, the players at love
On a square no bigger than a carpet

Are hustled over the crests and troughs,
Each stalled in his particular minute
And castled in it like a king.
Small drops spot their coats, their gloves:
They fly too fast to feel the wet.
Anything can happen where they are going.

The untidy lady revivalist
For whom the good Lord provides·(He gave
Her a pocketbook, a pearl hatpin
And seven winter coats last August)
Prays under her breath that she may save
The art students in West Berlin.

The astrologer at her elbow (a Leo)
Picked his trip-date by the stars.
He is gratified by the absence of icecakes.
He'll be rich in a year (and he should know)
Selling the Welsh and English mothers
Nativities at two and six.

And the white-haired jeweler from Denmark is carving
A perfectly faceted wife to wait
On him hand and foot, quiet as a diamond.
Moony balloons tied by a string
To their owners' wrists, the light dreams float
To be let loose at news of land.

Whitsun

This is not what I meant:
Stucco arches, the banked rocks sunning in rows,
Bald eyes or petrified eggs,
Grownups coffined in stockings and jackets,
Lard-pale, sipping the thin
Air like a medicine.

The stopped horse on his chromium pole
Stares through us; his hooves chew the breeze.
Your shirt of crisp linen
Bloats like a spinnaker. Hat-brims
Deflect the watery dazzle; the people idle
As if in hospital.

I can smell the salt, all right.
At our feet, the weed-mustachioed sea
Exhibits its glaucous silks,
Bowing and truckling like an old-school oriental.
You're no happier than I about it.
A policeman points out a vacant cliff

Green as a pool table, where cabbage butterflies
Peel off to sea as gulls do,
And we picnic in the death-stench of a hawthorn.
The waves pulse and pulse like hearts.
Beached under the spumy blooms, we lie
Seasick and fever-dry.

Zoo Keeper's Wife

I can stay awake all night, if need be—
Cold as an eel, without eyelids.
Like a dead lake the dark envelops me,
Blueblack, a spectacular plum fruit.
No air bubbles start from my heart. I am lungless
And ugly, my belly a silk stocking
Where the heads and tails of my sisters decompose.
Look, they are melting like coins in the powerful juices—

The spidery jaws, the spine bones bared for a moment
Like the white lines on a blueprint.
Should I stir, I think this pink and purple plastic
Guts bag would clack like a child's rattle,
Old grievances jostling each other, so many loose teeth.
But what do you know about that
My fat pork, my marrowy sweetheart, face-to-the-wall?
Some things of this world are indigestible.

You wooed me with the wolf-headed fruit bats
Hanging from their scorched hooks in the moist
Fug of the Small Mammal House.
The armadillo dozed in his sandbin
Obscene and bald as a pig, the white mice
Multiplied to infinity like angels on a pinhead
Out of sheer boredom. Tangled in the sweat-wet sheets
I remember the bloodied chicks and the quartered rabbits.

You checked the diet charts and took me to play
With the boa constrictor in the Fellow's Garden.
I pretended I was the Tree of Knowledge.
I entered your bible, I boarded your ark
With the sacred baboon in his wig and wax ears
And the bear-furred, bird-eating spider
Clambering round its glass box like an eight-fingered hand.
I can't get it out of my mind

How our courtship lit the tindery cages—
Your two-horned rhinoceros opened a mouth
Dirty as a bootsole and big as a hospital sink
For my cube of sugar: its bog breath
Gloved my arm to the elbow.
The snails blew kisses like black apples.
Nightly now I flog apes owls bears sheep
Over their iron stile. And still don't sleep.

Last Words

I do not want a plain box, I want a sarcophagus
With tigery stripes, and a face on it
Round as the moon, to stare up.
I want to be looking at them when they come
Picking among the dumb minerals, the roots.
I see them already—the pale, star-distance faces.
Now they are nothing, they are not even babies.
I imagine them without fathers or mothers, like the first gods.
They will wonder if I was important.
I should sugar and preserve my days like fruit!
My mirror is clouding over—
A few more breaths, and it will reflect nothing at all.
The flowers and the faces whiten to a sheet.

I do not trust the spirit. It escapes like steam
In dreams, through mouth-hole or eye-hole. I can't stop it.
One day it won't come back. Things aren't like that.
They stay, their little particular lusters
Warmed by much handling. They almost purr.
When the soles of my feet grow cold,
The blue eye of my turquoise will comfort me.
Let me have my copper cooking pots, let my rouge pots
Bloom about me like night flowers, with a good smell.
They will roll me up in bandages, they will store my heart
Under my feet in a neat parcel.
I shall hardly know myself. It will be dark,
And the shine of these small things sweeter than the face
        of Ishtar.

Black Rook in Rainy Weather

On the stiff twig up there
Hunches a wet black rook
Arranging and rearranging its feathers in the rain.
I do not expect a miracle
Or an accident

To set the sight on fire
In my eye, nor seek
Any more in the desultory weather some design,
But let spotted leaves fall as they fall,
Without ceremony, or portent.

Although, I admit, I desire,
Occasionally, some backtalk
From the mute sky, I can't honestly complain:
A certain minor light may still
Leap incandescent

Out of kitchen table or chair
As if a celestial burning took
Possession of the most obtuse objects now and then—
Thus hallowing an interval
Otherwise inconsequent

By bestowing largesse, honor,
One might say love. At any rate, I now walk
Wary (for it could happen
Even in this dull, ruinous landscape); sceptical,
Yet politic; ignorant

Of whatever angel may choose to flare
Suddenly at my elbow. I only know that a rook
Ordering its black feathers can so shine
As to seize my senses, haul
My eyelids up, and grant

A brief respite from fear
Of total neutrality. With luck,
Trekking stubborn through this season
Of fatigue, I shall
Patch together a content

Of sorts. Miracles occur,
If you care to call those spasmodic
Tricks of radiance miracles. The wait's begun again,
The long wait for the angel,
For that rare, random descent.

Metaphors

I'm a riddle in nine syllables,
An elephant, a ponderous house,
A melon strolling on two tendrils.
O red fruit, ivory, fine timbers!
This loaf's big with its yeasty rising.
Money's new-minted in this fat purse.
I'm a means, a stage, a cow in calf.
I've eaten a bag of green apples,
Boarded the train there's no getting off.

Maudlin

Mud-mattressed under the sign of the hag
In a clench of blood, the sleep-talking virgin
Gibbets with her curse the moon's man,
Faggot-bearing Jack in his crackless egg:

Hatched with a claret hogshead to swig
He kings it, navel-knit to no groan,
But at the price of a pin-stitched skin
Fish-tailed girls purchase each white leg.

Ouija

It is a chilly god, a god of shades,
Rises to the glass from his black fathoms.
At the window, those unborn, those undone
Assemble with the frail paleness of moths,
An envious phosphorescence in their wings.
Vermilions, bronzes, colors of the sun
In the coal fire will not wholly console them.
Imagine their deep hunger, deep as the dark
For the blood-heat that would ruddle or reclaim.
The glass mouth sucks blood-heat from my forefinger.
The old god dribbles, in return, his words.

The old god, too, writes aureate poetry
In tarnished modes, maundering among the wastes,
Fair chronicler of every foul declension.
Age, and ages of prose, have uncoiled
His talking whirlwind, abated his excessive temper
When words, like locusts, drummed the darkening air
And left the cobs to rattle, bitten clean.
Skies once wearing a blue, divine hauteur
Ravel above us, mistily descend,
Thickening with motes, to a marriage with the mire.

He hymns the rotten queen with saffron hair
Who has saltier aphrodisiacs
Than virgins' tears. That bawdy queen of death,
Her wormy couriers are at his bones.
Still he hymns juice of her, hot nectarine.
I see him, horny-skinned and tough, construe
What flinty pebbles the ploughblade upturns
As ponderable tokens of her love.
He, godly, doddering, spells
No succinct Gabriel from the letters here
But floridly, his amorous nostalgias.

Two Sisters of Persephone

Two girls there are: within the house
One sits; the other, without.
Daylong a duet of shade and light
Plays between these.

In her dark wainscotted room
The first works problems on
A mathematical machine.
Dry ticks mark time

As she calculates each sum.
At this barren enterprise
Rat-shrewd go her squint eyes,
Root-pale her meager frame.

Bronzed as earth, the second lies,
Hearing ticks blown gold
Like pollen on bright air. Lulled
Near a bed of poppies,

She sees how their red silk flare
Of petalled blood
Burns open to sun's blade.
On that green altar

Freely become sun's bride, the latter
Grows quick with seed.
Grass-couched in her labor's pride,
She bears a king. Turned bitter

And sallow as any lemon,
The other, wry virgin to the last,
Goes graveward with flesh laid waste,
Worm-husbanded, yet no woman.

Who

The month of flowering's finished. The fruit's in,
Eaten or rotten. I am all mouth.
October's the month for storage.

This shed's fusty as a mummy's stomach:
Old tools, handles and rusty tusks.
I am at home here among the dead heads.

Let me sit in a flowerpot,
The spiders won't notice.
My heart is a stopped geranium.

If only the wind would leave my lungs alone.
Dogsbody noses the petals. They bloom upside down.
They rattle like hydrangea bushes.

Mouldering heads console me,
Nailed to the rafters yesterday:
Inmates who don't hibernate.

Cabbageheads: wormy purple, silver-glaze,
A dressing of mule ears, mothy pelts, but green-hearted,
Their veins white as porkfat.

O the beauty of usage!
The orange pumpkins have no eyes.
These halls are full of women who think they are birds.

This is a dull school.
I am a root, a stone, an owl pellet,
Without dreams of any sort.

Mother, you are the one mouth
I would be a tongue to. Mother of otherness
Eat me. Wastebasket gaper, shadow of doorways.

I said: I must remember this, being small.
There were such enormous flowers,
Purple and red mouths, utterly lovely.

The hoops of blackberry stems made me cry.
Now they light me up like an electric bulb.
For weeks I can remember nothing at all.

Dark House

This is a dark house, very big.
I made it myself,
Cell by cell from a quiet corner,
Chewing at the grey paper,
Oozing the glue drops,
Whistling, wiggling my ears,
Thinking of something else.

It has so many cellars,
Such eelish delvings!
I am round as an owl,
I see by my own light.
Any day I may litter puppies
Or mother a horse. My belly moves.
I must make more maps.

These marrowy tunnels!
Moley-handed, I eat my way.
All-mouth licks up the bushes
And the pots of meat.
He lives in an old well,
A stoney hole. He's to blame.
He's a fat sort.

Pebble smells, turnipy chambers.
Small nostrils are breathing.
Little humble loves!
Footlings, boneless as noses,
It is warm and tolerable
In the bowel of the root.
Here's a cuddly mother.

Maenad

Once I was ordinary:
Sat by my father's bean tree
Eating the fingers of wisdom.
The birds made milk.
When it thundered I hid under a flat stone.

The mother of mouths didn't love me.
The old man shrank to a doll.
O I am too big to go backward:
Birdmilk is feathers,
The bean leaves are dumb as hands.

This month is fit for little.
The dead ripen in the grapeleaves.
A red tongue is among us.
Mother, keep out of my barnyard,
I am becoming another.

Dog-head, devourer:
Feed me the berries of dark.
The lids won't shut. Time
Unwinds from the great umbilicus of the sun
Its endless glitter.

I must swallow it all.

Lady, who are these others in the moon's vat—
Sleepdrunk, their limbs at odds?
In this light the blood is black.
Tell me my name.

The Beast

He was bullman earlier,
King of the dish, my lucky animal.
Breathing was easy in his airy holding.
The sun sat in his armpit.
Nothing went moldy. The little invisibles
Waited on him hand and foot.
The blue sisters sent me to another school.
Monkey lived under the dunce cap.
He kept blowing me kisses.
I hardly knew him.

He won't be got rid of:
Mumblepaws, teary and sorry,
Fido Littlesoul, the bowel's familiar.
A dustbin's enough for him.
The dark's his bone.
Call him any name, he'll come to it.

Mud-sump, happy sty-face.
I've married a cupboard of rubbish.
I bed in a fish puddle.
Down here the sky is always falling.
Hogwallow's at the window.
The star bugs won't save me this month.
I housekeep in Time's gut-end
Among emmets and mollusks,
Duchess of Nothing,
Hairtusk's bride.

Witch Burning

In the marketplace they are piling the dry sticks.
A thicket of shadows is a poor coat. I inhabit
The wax image of myself, a doll's body.
Sickness begins here: I am a dartboard for witches.
Only the devil can eat the devil out.
In the month of red leaves I climb to a bed of fire.

It is easy to blame the dark: the mouth of a door,
The cellar's belly. They've blown my sparkler out.
A black-sharded lady keeps me in a parrot cage.
What large eyes the dead have!
I am intimate with a hairy spirit.
Smoke wheels from the beak of this empty jar.

If I am a little one, I can do no harm.
If I don't move about, I'll knock nothing over. So I said,
Sitting under a potlid, tiny and inert as a rice grain.
They are turning the burners up, ring after ring.
We are full of starch, my small white fellows. We grow.
It hurts at first. The red tongues will teach the truth.

Mother of beetles, only unclench your hand:
I'll fly through the candle's mouth like a singeless moth.
Give me back my shape. I am ready to construe the days
I coupled with dust in the shadow of a stone.
My ankles brighten. Brightness ascends my thighs.
I am lost, I am lost, in the robes of all this light.

A Life

Touch it: it won't shrink like an eyeball,
This egg-shaped bailiwick, clear as a tear.
Here's yesterday, last year—
Palm-spear and lily distinct as flora in the vast
Windless threadwork of a tapestry.

Flick the glass with your fingernail:
It will ping like a Chinese chime in the slightest air stir
Though nobody in there looks up or bothers to answer.
The inhabitants are light as cork,
Every one of them permanently busy.

At their feet, the sea waves bow in single file.
Never trespassing in bad temper:
Stalling in midair,
Short-reined, pawing like paradeground horses.
Overhead, the clouds sit tasseled and fancy

As Victorian cushions. This family
Of valentine faces might please a collector:
They ring true, like good china.

Elsewhere the landscape is more frank.
The light falls without letup, blindingly.

A woman is dragging her shadow in a circle
About a bald hospital saucer.
It resembles the moon, or a sheet of blank paper
And appears to have suffered a sort of private blitzkrieg.
She lives quietly

With no attachments, like a foetus in a bottle,
The obsolete house, the sea, flattened to a picture
She has one too many dimensions to enter.
Grief and anger, exorcised,
Leave her alone now.

The future is a grey seagull
Tattling in its cat-voice of departure, departure.
Age and terror, like nurses, attend her,
And a drowned man, complaining of the great cold,
Crawls up out of the sea.

Crossing the Water

Black lake, black boat, two black, cut-paper people.
Where do the black trees go that drink here?
Their shadows must cover Canada.

A little light is filtering from the water flowers.
Their leaves do not wish us to hurry:
They are round and flat and full of dark advice.

Cold worlds shake from the oar.
The spirit of blackness is in us, it is in the fishes.
A snag is lifting a valedictory, pale hand;

Stars open among the lilies.
Are you not blinded by such expressionless sirens?
This is the silence of astounded souls.

71 72 73 10 9 8 7 6 5 4 3 2 1